GW00363882

Family Prayers

Selected by
Tricia Oliver

Illustrated by
Lyn Ellis

For Stephanie
my cousin and friend

First published in Great Britain in 1992
PALM TREE
Rattlesden, Bury St Edmunds
Suffolk IP30 0SZ
England

Lutheran Publishing House
205 Halifax Street
Adelaide
SA 5000
Australia

ISBN 0 86208 175 0

Printed in Hong Kong
by Colorcraft Limited

Contents

Love And Joy

Live within my love.
When you obey me you are
living in my love,
just as I obey my Father
and live in his love.
I have told you this so that
you will be filled with joy.
Yes, your cup of joy will overflow!

JOHN 15:9-11

Bless Our Home

Bless our home, Father,
that we cherish the bread
before there is none,
discover each other
before we leave,
and enjoy each other
for what we are,
while we have time.

Prayer Of Francis Of Assisi

Lord, make me an instrument
of your peace:
where there is hatred,
let me sow love:
where there is injury, pardon:
where there is doubt, faith:
where there is darkness, light:
where there is despair, hope,
and where there is sadness, joy.

Give Me Patience

It isn't in the quiet,
in the solitude of the study,
that I grow, Lord,
rather at the supermarket checkout
or behind a hopeless traffic jam.
Give me the deep breath of calm
when the clock is racing.

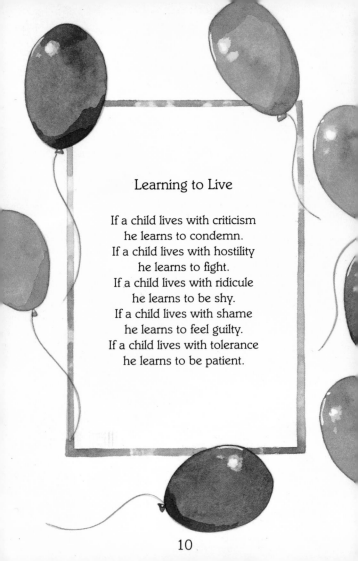

Learning to Live

If a child lives with criticism
he learns to condemn.
If a child lives with hostility
he learns to fight.
If a child lives with ridicule
he learns to be shy.
If a child lives with shame
he learns to feel guilty.
If a child lives with tolerance
he learns to be patient.

If a child lives with encouragement
he learns confidence.
If a child lives with praise
he learns to appreciate.
If a child lives with fairness
he learns justice.
If a child lives with security
he learns to have faith.
If a child lives with approval
he learns to like himself.
If a child lives with acceptance
and friendship
he learns to find love in the world.

11

If I Could

If I could, I would teach each child to be positive,
to smile, to love and be loved.

I would teach each child to take time
to observe some miracle of nature –
the song of a bird,
the beauty of a snowflake,
the orange glow of a winter sunset.

I would teach each child to feel warmly
about those for whom the task of learning
does not come easily.

I would teach each one to be kind
to all living creatures
and to crowd out of their lives
feelings of guilt, misunderstanding
and lack of compassion.

I would teach each child that it is alright
to show their feelings by laughing,
crying, or touching someone they care about.

Everyday I would have a child feel special
and through my actions,
each one would know how much
I really care.

We can do no great things,
only small things with great love.
MOTHER TERESA

Every work of love
brings a person
face to face
with God.
MOTHER TERESA

14

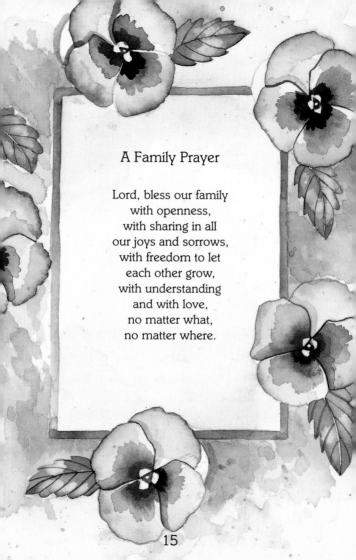

A Family Prayer

Lord, bless our family
with openness,
with sharing in all
our joys and sorrows,
with freedom to let
each other grow,
with understanding
and with love,
no matter what,
no matter where.

Safe Through The Night

Now I lay me down to sleep
I pray the Lord
my soul to keep,
and keep me safe
throughout the night,
and wake me
with the morning light.

At The Ending Of This Day

O Lord, my God,
I thank you at the ending of this day.
I thank you for rest of body and mind.
Your hand has been over me,
guarding and preserving me.
Forgive all my littleness of faith
and all the wrong I have done this day,
and help me to forgive all
who have done wrong to me.
Let me sleep in peace under your care.
I commit to you all whom I love,
all in this house,
and myself, both body and soul.
O God, praise be to your holy name.

Do not be anxious about anything,
by prayer and petition,
with thanksgiving
present your requests to God.
And the peace of God,
which transcends
all understanding,
will guard your hearts
and your minds
in Christ Jesus.

PHILIPPIANS 4:7

A Prayer When Distracted

When the heart is hard and parched up
come upon me with a shower of mercy.
When grace is lost from life
come with a burst of song.
When tumultuous work
raises its din on all sides
shutting me out from beyond
come to me, my Lord of silence,
with thy peace and rest.
When my beggarly heart sits crouched,
shut up in a corner,
break open the door
and come with the ceremony of a king.
When desire blinds the mind
with delusion and dust,
O thou holy one, thou wakeful,
come with thy light and thy thunder.

God Grant Me Serenity

God grant me SERENITY
to accept the things I cannot change,
COURAGE to change the things I can
and WISDOM to know the difference.

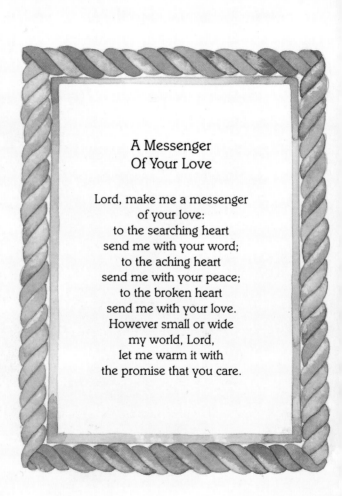

A Messenger
Of Your Love

Lord, make me a messenger
of your love:
to the searching heart
send me with your word;
to the aching heart
send me with your peace;
to the broken heart
send me with your love.
However small or wide
my world, Lord,
let me warm it with
the promise that you care.

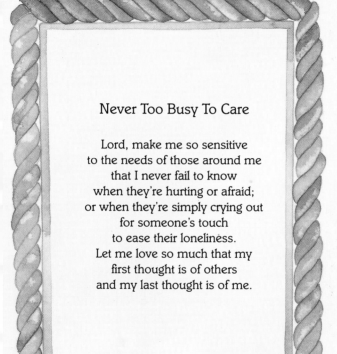

Never Too Busy To Care

Lord, make me so sensitive
to the needs of those around me
that I never fail to know
when they're hurting or afraid;
or when they're simply crying out
for someone's touch
to ease their loneliness.
Let me love so much that my
first thought is of others
and my last thought is of me.

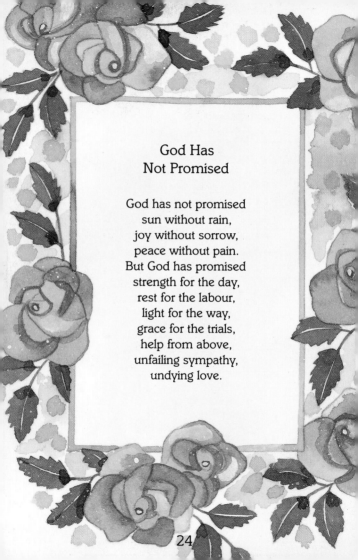

God Has
Not Promised

God has not promised
sun without rain,
joy without sorrow,
peace without pain.
But God has promised
strength for the day,
rest for the labour,
light for the way,
grace for the trials,
help from above,
unfailing sympathy,
undying love.

Remind me, Lord

Remind me, Lord, that your love
is bigger than any problem.
The more I look at the problem,
the bigger the problem becomes.
But when I look to you, Lord,
my anxiety pales
in the light of your love.

Kitchen Prayer

Lord of pots and pans and things,
since I've not time to be a saint
by doing lovely things,
or watching late with thee,
or dreaming in the dawn light,
or storming heaven's gates,
make me a saint by getting meals
and washing up the plates.
Although I must have Martha's hands,
I have a Mary mind,
and when I black the boots and shoes
thy sandals, Lord, I find.
I think of how they trod the earth
what time I scrub the floor;
accept this meditation, Lord,
I haven't time for more.

Together

Lord, help me remember
that nothing is going to happen today
that you and I cannot handle together.

Your Will For My Life

You know the deepest wishes
of my heart, Lord,
the cherished dreams,
the silent things,
for which I have no voice,
but better still is your will
for my life, Lord.
Let all that comes to me today
be those gifts of your choice.

Love

Love is patient and kind;
it is not jealous or conceited or proud;
Love is not ill-mannered
or selfish or irritable;
Love does not keep a record of wrongs;
Love is not happy with evil
but is happy with the truth.
Love never gives up;
and its faith, hope and patience
never fail.

I CORINTHIANS 13:4-7

The fruit of the Spirit is love,
joy, peace, gentleness, goodness,
faith, meekness, temperance.

GALATIANS 5:22-23

Be at peace with one another.

MARK 9:50

Jesus is pleased to come to us
as the truth to be told
and the life to be lived,
as the light to be lighted
and the love to be loved,
as the joy to be given
and the peace to be spread.

MOTHER TERESA

This is the confidence
which we have in him
that if we ask anything
according to his will
he hears us.

1 JOHN 5:14

A Family Prayer

Dear Father in heaven,
I ask for your touch,
bless all my family,
we need you so much.

Grant us your wisdom
to choose what is right,
to walk in your pathways
of truth and of light.

Strengthen our family
with faith to hold fast,
to cherish and nurture
the treasures that last.

Teach us to love,
to forgive and to share,
in the realms of the Spirit,
to thrive and to dare.

But most of all, Lord,
when our journey is through,
bind us together
for ever with you.

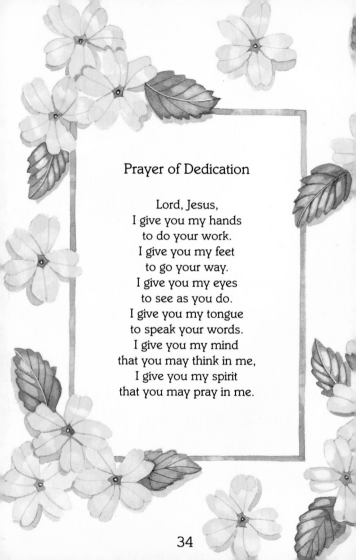

Prayer of Dedication

Lord, Jesus,
I give you my hands
to do your work.
I give you my feet
to go your way.
I give you my eyes
to see as you do.
I give you my tongue
to speak your words.
I give you my mind
that you may think in me,
I give you my spirit
that you may pray in me.

Above all
I give you my heart
that you may love in me,
your Father, and all mankind.
I give you my whole self
that you may grow in me,
so that it is you, Lord Jesus,
who live and work
and pray in me.

A Prayer for Patience

When my patience
seems too short
help me to stretch it;
teach me how to meet
a crisis with a smile.
When I'm running out
of quick and clever answers
let the questions stop
for just a while.

When it seems as though
the day has too few hours
in which to do the things
I have to do;
may I always find the time
for what's important –
time for listening,
time for love
and laughter too.

Love is a fruit in season
at all times.

MOTHER TERESA

Together we can
do something beautiful
for God.

MOTHER TERESA

38

The Day Returns

The day returns
and brings us the petty round
of irritating concerns and duties.
Help us to perform them
with laughter and kind faces.
Let cheerfulness
abound with industry.
Give us joy
in our business this day.
Bring us to our resting beds
weary and content
and undishonoured,
and grant us in the end
the gift of sleep.

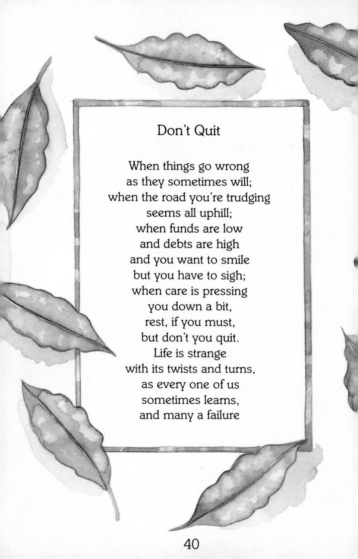

Don't Quit

When things go wrong
as they sometimes will;
when the road you're trudging
seems all uphill;
when funds are low
and debts are high
and you want to smile
but you have to sigh;
when care is pressing
you down a bit,
rest, if you must,
but don't you quit.
Life is strange
with its twists and turns,
as every one of us
sometimes learns,
and many a failure

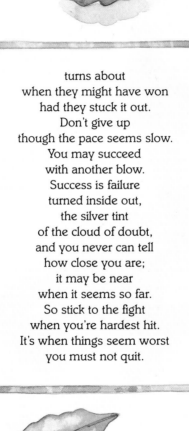

turns about
when they might have won
had they stuck it out.
Don't give up
though the pace seems slow.
You may succeed
with another blow.
Success is failure
turned inside out,
the silver tint
of the cloud of doubt,
and you never can tell
how close you are;
it may be near
when it seems so far.
So stick to the fight
when you're hardest hit.
It's when things seem worst
you must not quit.

Recipe for a Happy Home

Combine happy hearts,
melt hearts into one,
add a lot of love.
Mix well with respect.
Add gentleness, laughter, joy,
faith, hope and self-control.
Pour in much understanding.
Don't forget the patience.
Blend in listening ears.
Allow to grow and share.
Sprinkle with smiles, hugs and kisses.
Bake for a lifetime.
Yield: One Happy Home!

An Everyday Prayer

Lord, in all I do today,
remind me that there's just one way
to do the things that I do best,
to put my mind and heart at rest.
And that's to put in your great hands
my life, that you alone have planned.

Make me Willing

When I want to do
only great things, Lord,
make me willing to do
small, unnoticed things too.
When I want to do
what the world will acclaim,
make me willing to do
what will lift up your name.

Wherever you go
be a carrier of God's love.
MOTHER TERESA.

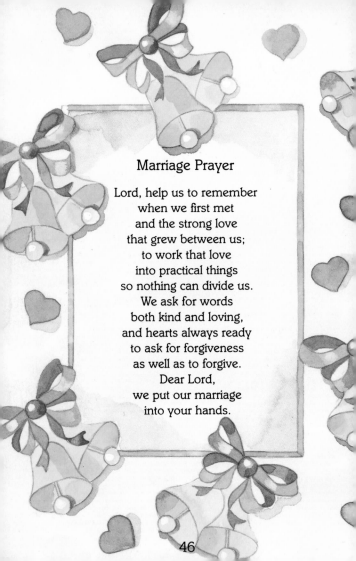

Marriage Prayer

Lord, help us to remember
when we first met
and the strong love
that grew between us;
to work that love
into practical things
so nothing can divide us.
We ask for words
both kind and loving,
and hearts always ready
to ask for forgiveness
as well as to forgive.
Dear Lord,
we put our marriage
into your hands.

Guide for a Loving Home

May we treat one another
with respect, honesty and care.
May we share the little discoveries
and changes each day brings.
May we try always to be sensitive
to one another's joys, sorrows,
needs and changing moods,
and realise that being
a loving family means
sometimes not understanding
everyone all the time
but being there to love
and help them just the same.

47

Simple acts of love and care
keep the light of Christ burning.

MOTHER TERESA